the infant vine

Isabella G. Mead was born in Hobart in 1989 and grew up in Melbourne. She is a PhD candidate in Creative Writing at Monash University and holds a BA from the University of Melbourne and an MA (Digital Humanities) from King's College London. Her work has been published widely, including in *Meanjin, Island, Westerly* and *Cordite Poetry Review*. In 2023, she was shortlisted twice for the Gwen Harwood Poetry Prize. She lives, works and raises her young family on unceded Wurundjeri land. *The Infant Vine* (UWA Publishing, July 2024) is her debut poetry collection.

the infant vine
Isabella G. Mead

UWA PUBLISHING

First published in 2024 by
UWA Publishing
Crawley, Western Australia 6009
www.uwap.uwa.edu.au

UWAP is an imprint of UWA Publishing
a division of The University of Western Australia

THE UNIVERSITY OF
WESTERN
AUSTRALIA

ISBN: 978-176080-286-8

A catalogue record for this
book is available from the
National Library of Australia

Cover design by Lisa White
Typeset in Joanna Nova by Lasertype
Printed by Lightning Source

 uwapublishing

For Clover and Hugo

You kiss the forehead — to wipe away memory.
I kiss the forehead.

Marina Tsvetaeva,
translated by Michael M. Naydan

Then all a world I made in me;
all the world you hear and see
hung up upon my dreaming blood.

Judith Wright

Contents

The Green Wedge

I am walking the river's slow edge
with my daughter tucked, frog-legged,
in a sun-faded carrier.

Despite appearances she is mammal
to a tee. She snuffles, nuzzles
my chest like a truffle dog

the loamy earth. On the bank
I position her latch
with my framer's hands.

She drinks deeply, a memory
restores—oars muscling
through water, the stroke

of a welcome swallow's wing
mid-flight. Birds instruct
in lapsed song *mine* and *here*

and *yours*. My daughter pulls
off, grabs my arm in her soft fist.
Breath reverses in an undergrowth

teeming with planet-heavy ants.
There is so much we don't see—
frogs tenanting yellow marsh-flowers,

a glimmer of eggs cradled
in the slick tympanum of pondweed.
The sun softens in brown water,

reeds beget reeds. Lifting
my daughter to face the river,
its surface corrugated with milfoil,

her springform legs kick
against the heel of my heart.
What will remain? Frogs or birds,

the unsteady march of ants?
Let it be more than loose stones
bargaining at the mouth,

the hatching of a lone tadpole
like a clammy jolt of love.

Personal Slalom

my daughter is born in February
the yellow month   sun-
fried grass   scent of tomato stalks
slim cream flowers   she wakes before dawn
hungry as a house cat   her cry splits milk
twists eyes from sleep   I carry her down
where the air is cooler   the winter olympics
playing out   in white-and-gold
on television: an alpine arena
skiers bending like saplings   on a steep hill
I place her across   the soft uneven
plain of my stomach   greet her apple bobbing mouth
with an intake of breath   the harsh chh
when a skier takes   a corner sharply
between bright flags   they spray snow
when my milk comes in   I feel it in my molars
she drinks like a tiny sailor   pushes and pulls
tissue and skin   with soft fists
skiers shave   seconds off
a green clock   all I think about is
bodies   why some choose
to careen theirs   down mountains
the cut   and the let-down
the apparatus of want   and give-
take   how my skeleton curves
to lift ceaselessly   the small life falling
asleep in my arms   between two lungs
blue gates   on the slalom

Night Notes

i.

When C is born, I use my Notes app to tap out loosely twined drafts. A slender maze appears on a drive. Blank files multiply. One is labelled 'rage', another 'baby socks'. Exhaustion scuppers any attempt to retrieve memory from song or the day-before. Silence punctuated by tiny arms un-swaddling: the escapologist loosening the tucked edges of muslin like a dream lifting from its small box. My breath a commash. My breath holding & held in the heft of another's sleep. In the stuffy quiet of 3am, eyes gritty with fatigue, I start a new file—'Notes2'—document in vacant folders the precious unlit hours.

ii.

When H is born, I listen to white noise & pretend I am driftwood on grey water. My insides slip inside the hollow that once held him. I don't write. Not a word. I lie & will myself to sleep, to be as dull & dulled as driftwood on greyest water, all my knots smoothed over. Hours in & out like the tide. H grunts & from his swaddle frees his balled hands, which he sucks with barnacle-vigour. The more he wriggles & squirms the stiller I become—a driftwood has no arms. Has barely a body.

iii.

When one tries to commit to memory, the other tries to forget. & vice-versa. & on-and-on. The mind wants to remember it—the body wants to erase it. Wants to zip it. The body craves its joy—the mind lets it slip. I am so tired I am in-between myself. There is no laughter in the twilight of deprivation, only a crackling sound. A typeface ashy from disuse. I re-write the same line. When my body remembers sleep, my mind forgets it—then compensates for this loss by working overtime. No one works harder than the mind denied sleep—no one. I write it down somewhere. I take it up with the sun.

The Scar

In the aftermath, my friend asks me
how I will explain the scar to C.

Could you say it was a shark bite?
She's not serious but I consider it anyway—

the shark, arrow tipped in brown iodine,
blood-trained. Narrow eyes focus

like a needle trailing red silk. Later, my hands
attend the honeycomb dressing. Each gauzed

hexagon gleams—the wound below a gummy smile
thinning into permanence. Of course, the story

won't hold water—the scar a ruled line and not
a cartoon flower chomp. Its precision studied,

the opposite of any creature born from a salt purse.
C wouldn't believe me anyway.

See how she observes my lips as I speak?
The direction of my gaze will give me away—

not out to sea but directly ahead, eye to blue
eye. She'll recognise it at once. Her personal

entry point—tissue-white, tensile as a diving board.

Bonnethead

i.

The phones break apart in the night.
Hands grind news into moon-split bitumen,
headlines merge with blue light. In the morning
your neighbour, M, returns from her seaside sojourn.
She passes you a gift—a shell the size of your palm.
You know the disease is in you by the afternoon.
It is in the way you taste, running your tongue along
the roof of your mouth, the accumulation of dreams—
silt and sand in old cells, coiled rooms resurrecting
pearls in the shape of wrenches. A week passes.
Heat settles over a city scored by fear. In filed streets
your boyfriend hurls a stone, protests effacement.
Pro-lifers stew in half-light, doubtful for once.
When the skies open, rain progresses rivers,
seas rise like welts. From shorelines the water takes
on a reddish hue. M says there are more of you every day.

ii.

O to be cartilaginous! Multiplying!
Your legs made for swimming, your lungs for holding
air in airless places. Under soft skirts you hide
your stomach, smooth fabric over skin like a mouth
over joy, curving the crumb of it. M, furtive now,
buys deli meats, ripe and fragrant stone fruit.
She leaves cantaloupe halves by your door
with a note scrawled in blue ink, not long now!
You notice the excess of o, the undone n. Returning
to the empty tub where you have taken to sleeping,
you see a square of yellow light resembles a fish tank.

Milk and brine on your tongue—two eggs appear,
shell-less, fig-sized. Pearlescent daughter shapes
swim beneath their surface, shadows in apple-white
albumin. The mother in you beams.

iii.
Washing dishes, you are submerged elbow-deep
in sea foam. In sleep you hatch amber dreams.
Waking, see green—visions of seagrass meadows,
vast and abundant kelp beds. Your boyfriend grows
suspicious when you cannot stop smiling, withdraws
without a word. In imprinted silence, you open the door
to M. She shows you her own, fulsome and nacreous.
You drink from fluted glasses as the news plays out
in hushed and wondrous tones. Footage of estuaries.
Magnified double helices like ornamental stairwells
plunging into vaulted surf. A reporter grins as she
removes her shoes, digs her toes deeply into sand.

iv.
In another ocean a bonnethead hunts for an empty
stretch of water. In her mind's ovaline eye—
a brood of daughters lined up like teeth.

Note
The bonnethead belongs to the shark genus Sphyrna. It is one of the few species
of sharks in which parthenogenesis, a form of asexual reproduction, has been
confirmed. It is also the only shark known to be omnivorous.

Becoming a Leafy Seadragon on the Birth of My Daughter

after a depth of nine metres: a Leafy Seadragon (image by Andrew Bowie, Australian Museum)

Leafy

not yet all-leaf but close—   flourishing

flesh   tones, kelp-like mass.

My hands   are rushes, my mouth a   hush.

At home I appear to drift   expertly between

rooms: a floating display.   How could I have known?

My body, its mounds of amber,   mythical lobes, buoying

the baby   not leafy like me   but sleek   and rose-round—

seal pup   of dreams, softly   restored when slept in my arms.

I shimmer with   effort, turn   the colour of walls.

Serenity   an illusion. See my neck-fins work very hard, work

overtime   in the deep-water dark of two a.m., propelling another body

toward   satiety and sleep.

The rest is camouflage. Be dazzled when I disappear into creaks,

into bed   frames and chests of pine drawers. Below a surface

before a mirror   I am my inverse–   toughened, sexless.

My hardened   spine menaces   sharks,   the long

eye of a camera.   Outside where trees sprout

like forgotten pier posts, I see my fellow leafy ones.

Tufted   yellow-green   gills

give us away every time. We smile as we pass

wearily trailing   our rigid silk,

sargassum,

saltwater.

Our babies

more beautiful than

you can be-

lieve

Megafauna

range the pages, large as houses. A scale for each
terraced species—megafauna:man. How small

we are. How puny and decorative our limbs.
I point out the regulars—richly fanged smilodon,

mammoths in their wiry woollens. Less familiar
are the lumbering megaherbivores devouring

sweet malus, elasmotherium bowing their heads
beneath the weight of myth. You ask me how

one becomes extinct. I fumble for answers,
look to the ground sloth inching in furred skin,

the dream-like giant otters playing like grown children
in rivers of regular size. Starve, maladapt, get eaten.

I don't want to talk about any of it. If only ratio
was the most interesting plot, paraceratherium

could continue on, heads figured like kites caught
in the branches of tall trees. If I must explain

extinction then I also need to mention endurance.
A body's devotion. How the mother cave bear

stripped leaves from branches, fossicked for tubers
in the cold ground. That she might somehow hear me

when I speak of death—hers and ours—and move
her bones as if to the distant growl of thunder.

I can count the number of years you have existed
on one hand: a fraction of a nanosecond chipped off

its planetary timescale. Something very small, very
brief is gathering. I am reading this book to you

and have failed to note the sixth mass extinction.
I will have to tell you another day. For now I can say,

with certainty, that memory catenates. Light dedicates
its photons to eyes. Extant in sound or atmosphere,

in the tides of this planet's blue oceans, an imprint—
a ferrying of cubs across a low, grassy plain.

Anorthite

after anorthite, primary mineral [sample held by the National Museum of Natural
History]

The moon is knocked out of the sky today.   Later, some will claim they
heard it: soft clap of distant thunder,   deep vibration like the breamed
face of a cliff falling into the sea.   In actuality, it sounds like nothing.
Or everything: a continuation.   This is Wednesday: rhyme time at the
library. I bounce A on my lap   and sing the familiar songs. Mid-merrily
a mother shrieks, holds   her phone high into the air. On its screen,
calamitous white fragments   twist like blasted fuselage through space.
Babies begin wailing in a word-   less call-and-response. The librarian
falters, arms extended to pull   imaginary oars fall silently to his side. I
grab A and hide in a quieter aisle,   buffeted by books on lifestyle and
interior design. I try to call my mother,   but she does not answer. When
I call L, he picks up only to say he is in   a meeting and cannot talk. We
stay crouched like this for a long time.   The baby grows bored and
grabs at me with her small, needful hands.   When we exit the building,
the streets are quiet. People stand gazing at   the sky, their mouths
open like sun-seeking flowers. Looking up, I see   only blue amongst
light-raked clouds. At home I feel the floor pitch;   A wriggles backwards
onto the plush rug. I want to focus on the words   splintering the screen:
a red timeline of breaking and this now in,   but my attention falters,
wounded. I wonder: will today be the day   A masters crawling? I see
her slanted hand-knee amble gain speed   and traction. I press my
fingers into my eyes and the rubble of the day   appears before me: how
we might forever recall progress with   concomitant disaster. I pick her
up, whisper, not today, and place her   in a bee-striped bouncer. For
dinner I cube and boil a pumpkin,   mash it into a smooth orange paste.
The baby eats gladly with her   balled hands. The voice of a newsreader
speaks to the room. Here   is a man accustomed to tallies and terror;
still his voice trembles.   *Devastation to tidal ecosystems— Earth*

wobble— Our ability   to survive— Accidental or deliberate? The debate
swirls like wreckage.   At six L arrives home in a flurry. He kisses A's
head then grips   my shoulders in a way that is intended to convey
something. *Sorry   I'm late. Traffic was crazy.* L wipes a damp cloth
over the baby's   face. She smiles widely so that we witness the resinous
entirety of   her mouth. From the gum, a single tooth gleams. L and I
look at each   other with horror. We are thinking the same thing: how
similar that   first peg of quartzy enamel is to lunar rock. Above us the
dented   solar system sweeps up its rich debris. We consider our lives
on an   axial tilt and run a warm bath for A.

Fool at Perigee

In making the image, the once-lusty moon
is cancelled out by twice-borrowed light. Chip
from a nicked saucer, splintered tooth in my palm—
porcelain when I was going for vaster rock
touched by ice, blue as it floats like a petrified jelly
in the pelagic sky. Or lilac at the very least,
stained by a soft winter sunset. I text my mother,
check out the moon. By the time she replies, a crowd
of clouds have eaten it like a preshow snack.

> O *wafer*
> O *mouth of ours*

When I see the moon I reach for my phone,
extract it from my bag like a decorative lorgnette.
The results of my enthusiasm—cruelly lit satellites,
discoloured sclera—flatten under scrutiny
like a celebrity crush. To my daughter I say, "look up!"
Taking her hand in mine, I point to a patch
of high indigo. "See the moon next to that socket-
shaped cloud?" Shaking me off, she skips ahead
in pink-and-aqua sneakers.

> O *cut out circle*
> O *left thumb cuticle*

This evening the moon is vast—a supermoon
according to the news. I snap three times.
The sudden unease when a large object vanishes.
Perhaps that last photo will be okay? No—
they are all terrible, the last one especially.

My girl, I know it is folly. I am filling distant servers
with clippings of light, impressions of fullness.
And for what? Not memory but a means to keep
that moon's cool, aseptic gaze on me—a stone I can
hold when records break and the dry grass dries.

> O *auto* focus
> O *face* of thine

So What's Your Ideal Dinner Party

and I'm off like a bear turning her huge velvety head to the distant
twitch of a rabbit's ears. Ideally it's not a party but an occasion for
solemn silence as the house is dismantled, reduced to bare earth
hedged by maidenhair ferns. In this peppery green ditch where no
one can see or hear me, I shun silver flatware, the fussiness of knives.
The only tool I need is a serving spoon, carved—like this hour—by my
own hand. The food will be soaked and roasted and cloven with spice.
Peaches and cherries slicked by fire; bread with a colossal, planetary
crust. I close my eyes as I eat. I won't be interrupted, no small hand
will skim my meal. I refuse all guests, even the famous ones; especially
the dead ones. There will be no music, only the sound of an ocean
moving against a far off shore. In expensive silence I subsume each
tasty atom. The pursuit is purely personal, immensely selfish: I won't
share, won't even look a cloud in the eye.

Dinnertime

after Madeline Donahue's 'Gleaner' (2022)

The long slide from upright to
    sidelong to floored for the morsel
        of choice—one striped, floss-pink rasher.

A table's surface is finite. No match
    for the flaxen-haired child who throws
        his green veg high into the air like spring-

time confetti. We eye the errant pea,
    the cups that tip and spill and need
        refilling for the thousandth time. Blue

water is pouring itself out as if the source
    is a broken faucet and not a wayward elbow.
        The detritus has a name—dinner.

Slicked plates revel in spillage. At five pm
    they clatter and roister in the mild hands
        of children. How close they are to shattering!

The Human Body

The river outgrows its bank like a child her shoes: incremental
then all at once. Our impulse to quench, to see in rain

a container for sweetness. On holiday we are water wheels
sluicing our hearts in a cold, dark stream. Seeking rows of soft reeds,

columns of cattail to spread our mouths, our limbs like green velvet.
Ouse, Esk, Beck, Lud. Curtly skirting the vowel, the o in go-on,

the rivers of your country don't need to say much to make
their point. The conclusion: leave well alone.

On the riverbank where water carves root from rock,
you light a slim fire, grill mushrooms wide as brimmed hats.

In fields of honeyed nettle we circle Bronze Age tumuli,
shower beneath silver branches. Alder or ash.

Sun-nets large enough to hold a flock of scuttled fish.
In the downpour a kettle hums thickly. Black tea, sugared loaf:

still life made unstill. We remove sodden layers in an evening,
let water pool in its valleys. The river in your hands, your tongue.

My hips, submerged, emerging. If a river is a promise
it's already broken. Years since we slept on Avon's misty bank,

hair damp with the climate. A new river furnishes a flood plain,
fills our eyes with sky-reflecting charms, birds in flight.

Dinghies are reported ferrying pet dogs and pregnant women.
Tan water delivers clouds of young mosquitoes: a rebirth.

The baby arrives in summer when the river drops.
Lawns erupt in yellow flowers, incautious, resolute. Rudderless

evenings spent fractious with fatigue, jagged with joy. A tumbler
of half-drunk water on every available surface. Our home:

accidental glass armonica. Baby-as-conductor. Or conduit
to the source. So who names a body of water? And what courage

is required? The only way to find out: dip our toes into cool,
brown water, dive below. Then come up, up into air.

Genesis

after Barbara Hepworth's 'Genesis' (1969), lithograph on paper

i.

Before wheat fields and orange groves,
before the black soil
and the slender grasses that grew from it:

a dust-up like a dance in slow-motion.

ii.

Compared to your own, a star nursery
is palatial. It harbours every colour.

In this haze vaulted to the nth degree,
planetesimal seeks planetesimal,
the thrill of collision, ergo expansion.

It should not surprise us that turbulence
gives birth to stars. Planets, too.
Hera, pushing away infant Heracles,
spills her milk. We tremble at the sight
of our lactic galaxy, story its source.

iii.

The first question to ask when expecting a baby
is not: *boy or girl?*
But: *spring, summer, autumn or winter?*

My firstborn is a summer baby. Her cry
calls in the sun so that for six long weeks
we sleep in a cradle of heat and cicada song.

When my second-born arrives
with autumn's cool ruffle,
we cover his head in soft amber wool.

Birth-weather as memory aid:
where were you when the earth opened up
and delivered heat and light
in a parcel of a candy-striped terry cotton?

iv.

Between worlds the air is warm and wet.
Spring, accustomed to bleating,
sprouts like a tender blue crown.

v.

The problem begins when we forget our births.
Trees ignite out of season.
Left unchecked, they blister and blaze
like baby stars.

Ash in the sky darkens the sun until
it appears bloody:
one born every minute, et cetera.

vi.

Though space is cold and often empty,
its largesse knows no bounds:

how a grain of dust can one day expand
to fit the whole world around its axis;
how the Orion Nebula contains green tint.

Despite its vastness, there is no place where
we would not find each other:
gravity's tug like a hand on my skirt,
your breath shaped to the bend of my ear.

vii.

Slowly and with exquisite drama:
motherhood as accretion, a gathering
of smaller bodies to larger ones.

Midwinterish

after 'Winter Solstice' (1970) by Barbara Hepworth, screenprint on paper

I. PINK

Out of each toffee apple, a small white bite. The children chew as
if they are babies again, tongues doing the work of teeth. When the
pink rind proves too difficult, they pass the stick back to me so that I
must eat the gummed fruit or else hold it for the evening, long after
the bonfire is lit. Three teenage girls are chanting, *light it up! Light it
up!* As the first orange flames begin climbing the mound like ants, my
daughter turns to me, suddenly afraid, and asks if we can go home. I
am not surprised: this is a child who grows uneasy when birthday
candles are lit. We move away from the fire but the sparks follow,
freewheeling high into the smoke-filled sky. *The fire can't hurt you,* I
say even as I doubt myself. The embers look hungry: a thousand hot
mouths. I take her sticky hand in mine until the air runs cold and
clear again.

II. BLUE

I wake early to small, heat-seeking hands. By 9am we are walking down
the high street, cold air nettling our faces. My son refuses his jacket,
says, *carry me,* by ceasing to walk. I say, *I'll carry you as far as the cafe.* Later,
I buy him a cinnamon donut which he eats in solemn silence. I sit and
watch because what else is there to do but witness his quiet, serious
pleasure, to brush, with the side of my finger, the fine powder of
bronzed sugar from his top lip.

Later, at the park, he watches another child beat mushrooms growing
up through woodchip. My son takes up his stick, yells, *gill the
mushrooms!* I direct his hand away and say, *no, don't kill the mushrooms.*
There is so much to learn. Every day we stuff our mouths with lessons:
this is/is not how we live. This is how mushrooms live. They explode

from the earth in a single night, impossibly soft, learn to submit to sunlight by morning's first rays.

At home, a gas provider emails me, *Isabella, stay toasty for less this winter.* I could be lonely. I could be lonelier except my son is an industry, a metropolis of needs, desires, personalities. He kicks off his shoes, wails when a sock gets stuck between ankle and heel. I teach him how to pinch and pull the cotton off. He is learning, very slowly. I cook pasta on the stovetop: dinosaur shapes that quickly lose their shape. My son does not mind formlessness. He eats with his fingers, says mm-mm-mm. I think that by summer, I will miss this ruffled and idling mid-June day.

III. MORE BLUE

This morning the sky is bluer than bottled water's plastic cap. I could be standing at the edge of a lake in a boreal forest where pink trout the size of bear snouts swim, my reflection creased by water. I see myself distorted but I suspect they do not. How my mother was a giant, once: a mountaintop covered in soft grasses, huffing out clouds. I want to explain that blue is a ritual, a repeating pattern that rewards attention. See how this sky has been following us all morning? It has been following me since I was born, a Spring squall, but I did not realise until now.

Today the sun will travel its shortest path but the sky will remain blue in ceremonial dispersion. The season dictates how we hold ourselves. Winter says, *let go of this and this and those.*

On the way to school my son trips and grazes his knee, the skin cross-hatched white and pink like freshly woven plaid. My daughter walks on without us. She has seen her friends. She is running toward the green school gate and won't be slowed. I tell my son that he will be alright. The body heals. If a scar remains, it is only another lesson. I kiss his appley fingers until he laughs and pulls away. I remind myself it is Winter Solstice, shortest day of the year, and he has so little time to wait.

.

Children's Literature

Whatever trace the fire left has cleared—the horizon
a habit, blue with distance. By morning
birdsong unsnarls cloud from cover, rainfall averages
in the knotted speech of clover. Footpaths redefine
in autumn's grand discard. Through shoals
of burnished plane you wade, shuttling a red reader
in a backpack half your size. Now you have learnt
the letters C, A, T, P, I, N, can sound out *ck* and *puh*
and *ee*. Animals learn to spell, too: field mice, first,
then dogs who wander far from home, muddying
their paws in speaking creeks. At night we read stories
about girls who turn into dragons, take to the sky,
embrace precious metals. Winged, newly clawed—
how easy it is to slough off one's girlhood,
reveal the glittery scales beneath. Your head resting
against my shoulder, hair damp with bathwater,
is pinkly scented with mock strawberry. I want to live
here—in amber. Delivered to a grassy peak, fearless
until the next evening when you ask,
            if we die, does the world start again?
Turning on taps, I lose the thread in the din of running
water. We sleep without dreaming, wake so early
your face swirls, planetary in morning's blue ink.

It is true there was a fire and it burnt a hole through
our imagination. One year ago, now two. There is no escape
in retelling. Overnight your hair pivots—blonde to maple-
brown. In a bluster of leaves, boots slick with uncollected
rain, you fashion stick-swords, long shields of paperbark.
The air carries a distant roar—winter's cold ruffle.

Everywhere your laughter spills its gilded hooks
into silent earth so that I must wonder if—like smoke—
        you've already moved on.

The Transfer

How is it possible to weigh more asleep
than awake? We're bound
by weird physics—after all that drag,
you were born mid-lift, brought into
pink relief high above my head.
Baby-turned-epiphyte. Grown
from my hip, strong and limber
as plant matter. From birth the desire
to remain upright persists: infant vine,
you thrash and wail if rested at an angle
of more than twenty degrees.
To fall asleep, you must be danced
to dappled music, a club beat:
Four Tet's *New Energy*. You are heaviest,
then: my shoulders ache and droop
as I spin you, miniature planet
with an iron core. Now when I lift you
from the car, weighted, perhaps, with
the effort of dreaming, I manoeuvre
my body to shade your face from the sun.
Eyelids flicker as I shimmy keys from
my bag, inch open the front door.
You grasp at wakefulness—the infringement
of a glowing ball on the periphery.
I hold my breath as you reach for it.
You miss the catch, drift back to sleep.
We breathe out on one. When I stand up,
your cut-out remains in the slope of
my back, the cave-in of my chest. From erosion

another self emerges, flattish, shaped
like a scapula. In the sturdy triangular bone:
a weather-proof shelter for two.

The Wing

after an image of moth wing scales, Kevin Mackenzie, Wellcome Collection

A mother's wing is very small. Too small
to excise or to see with the human eye.

Sometimes I feel mine straining
against my shirt. You may be wondering:

what good is a single, imperceptible wing?
It does not fly, it is not beautiful.

Scaled in leaf-prints. Soft like a snake's
rested body on the eve of summer.

I first noticed mine unfurling in theatre.
The doctors wore blue gowns and my eyes

filled with partition blue. I did not know
whether she lived or for how long,

and the wing fluttered to remind me
I was still a mother, had still given breath to

or in the world. And she did breathe:
the baby took in lungfuls of sweet air, became

pink with it. Even mothers who have lost
retain their wing. Too inured to chance

and unfavourable winds, too insubstantial
to be clipped. It comforted me, then, to know

no one could take it away. The wing
or the name that grew from me.

The First Week

At first we are startled by your pearly cry.
Air quivers with the force of new lungs,
takes on a mineral sheen. Think *oyster shell*.

Think *mother of*. Then the surprise of your mouth—
small hollow hedged by thirst. Daisy with a pink head.
Alert to circles, you shower in round shapes—

eye, breast, breakfast plate. We eat with gusto
as the morning shakes out like a blue sheet.
Your hands open, reveal plain daylight, close again.

Under the palm of another woman, you howl
an incredible pitch. I atone for the heel prick.
Blood-bead wiped by midwife's brisk.

Think *kitten*. No—think *eagle chick*. At home
you are unbridled and bidden, corralling the hours
when evening shucks off its sense-making light.

Lifting you resolves the simple need.
You drink and drink, roots alive to a wellspring.
Think *honeyeater*. Think nothing else but this

sharp sweetness. Sensate bloom. We bump nightly
against a delicate sphere. Sleep weaves in and out
of reach, dissolves on touch like the eyed wing of a moth.

A dance of part and parcel. A dream of folding
triangles. A day does not begin, it extends like an arm,
flexing the warm silver-flecked night. A seascape

encountered through a small grey box offers respite.
White noise machine—index of all known wave sounds.
Wave against rock. Wave against sand—shifting or glass.

Wave built upon the first wave. The desperate swell
of a wave without crest. You a summer baby
and the milk half-water. I eat salted eggs and ice chips,

tomatoes dunked in vinegar. Tender week old and the tang
of new life still smarts. What leaves a pale print.
Your cord stump—the body's crude caesura.

Think flotsam curled in ocean's slick churn. I marvel
at its emerald sheen, fortune's trinket or greenest
magic trick. The gristle that marks us both and mends.

I Cutlass Spent Days With an X

Question: *What does every ancient reef forget?*
Answer: *That time stopped for it several thousand years ago.*

The line—stain on a sundial's brow. Imprecise, fading outward.
Crowned by the earth's long furlough from heat and dust.

A hand paused at six o'clock—the hour that brightens the blue lawn,
threads steam from the kettle's mouth.

The self-same hour gathers like silt in a harbour where seabeds
nourish their fossils-to-be. I want to break open

each minute, eat the loose seconds where they fall.
At forty weeks the line is a rusted gnomon.

You swim in the noon gap—metal goldfish tocking the bowl.
Linea nigra. Watched pot. Each night you kick the line—

extensible, impatient to begin.

I Trial a Baby Sleep Journal

Wake and feed between one & two a.m.—
    Blast a phone to my eyes
    Will them open with feared blue light

Awake. Defend the meanest bite of sleep—
    Taste pink grit between my teeth
    Hold on until her hand's tiny proof moves against mine

Fended awake @ four forty-five a.m.—
    Fight off sleep while she drinks dreamless
    Cannot let her slip lest speechless rooms swallow her whole

Weaken—faded like a phone on low charge—
    Even though it is seven a.m. and the sun is streaming
    Its yellow streamers. Bliss is

A few kneaded minutes where we sleep together—
    Wake to her small doughy face
    Seven forty five a.m. when we rise

Interiors

Your voice hangs in the air gauzy with early summer heat.
Above us, a verse of birds weave half-learnt songs.
Prompted by their casual chat, you tell me how
a lorikeet flew inside a house and now it's Rosie's pet.

I consider the blow-in—blue-feathered head. Open window—
or was it a door? And who decided the bird would stay on?
The bird? I want to ask but you skip ahead. A fringe of bees
scud the verge, skim its sparse yellow flowers. Mynas scatter

over pavement where each driveway invites a chance encounter.
Flash of emerald feathers, belly of red. The driver invisible
behind light-scrummed glass when the wheel clips the curb.
Lit up in amber stoplight, you pause inches from the car.

Lungs stuffed with warm air, I breathe you out and out
                              and don't stop breathing.

The Quickening

To lie awake in darkness
is to listen to a dishwasher
cycling through its waters,
the thrum of cars on a sloped road.

Night hastens her movements,
rouses the gulf between us in black mallow.

As if on a tide she is brought to me—
over, under. Her twitch is my twitch.
I push her back, pull her in.

On rising, rest escapes pleasure,
takes root in necessary,
immobile ground.

The Near-Miss

is over yet clings to my skin for days.
Oil-coated, persistent as voice.

The time it takes to lift up a child into air—to pull her gasping
       from thickest water—
is one second halved,
halved again. I breathe life into each splinter,
animate the plunge in reverse.

Close shaves cost a slice of air.
Anybody with enough capillaries
can pay the small price. Change will not be given

but a lifetime guarantee
in the murmur of an asteroid's flight—
       calamities are commonplace.

Ode to a BabyCentre Forum

As in the inner workings of a hive, each is giving:
   each has taken a small piece. On the continuum
of *consoled—consoler*, roles are distributed

and advice imparted without expectation of reply.
   Like a flower's bright mouth to pollinators
no cry or question goes unanswered.

Fears dissected, worries unpicked softly by
   furred tongues. Every loss has a companion loss:
every loss is represented. When pain is catalogued,

sympathy extends like cold smoke by the moderators
   of loss. Observations that could mean nothing
or spell disaster are gathered and shared above

the common ground of loss. And when loss
   is beaten back by a tenacious wing stroke
on a favoured wind, joys are offered up: first flutter

to first kick and what to name the golden specks
   who float in studied waters. Held up to light
we begin to glint. Idle days roll by like fields

and second-timers give tips on provisions.
   When a storm hits, we assess the structure
of a home. Those who have already left devise

routes in air. The direction never changes:
   begin again. Sometimes it is a matter of how to
begin at all: raspberry leaf tea, clary sage, castor oil.

What to do when the blood does not stop. (We
    are so sorry for your loss). Each striving to pack
the place with sweetness enough to last a winter,

to recognise a dance-partner in a rectangle of light.

White Noise Machine Triptych

I [Rain]

Staticky maker of sleep—the white noise machine
loops rain/ river/ ocean/ from the bedside table.

Unless I count my own, my son has never seen a body of water.
A kind of baby-magic how he recognises a home-coming
in its lo-fi drip and churn.

He watches me mildly—sated and weary.
A state of anticipatory need that erupts in sucked cheeks,
a cry so impatient it hurries blood, outpaces
the water pooling about our feet.

II [River]

A tinnier sleep-song on turning the dial.
I lay his head in the brook of my arm, tilt him
as if he is a this-way-up box that must not get wet.

He chafes at the swaddle, our game of postie-and-parcel.
The mirage of slow-moving water cannot still
infant-thoughts turning this way and that
like a school of fish. He flounders in my arms,
anxious for saltwater.

I pop a heart-shaped in his wide pink mouth.
He spits it out—a sinker.
It is not a pacifier he wants but the Pacific,
to be a whale calf rolling in and out of blue surf.

III [Ocean]

In dark waters we charge forward.
My back bending to shield his body from brackish spray
is a dim sail.
Shearwaters forge a shortcut on a southerly gust
while a distant ship lumbers on, substantial with freight.

The moment I fear we might drown
or be dashed upon rocks,
his breathing steadies like a righted boat.

Evening settles like ash across a mantle.
I stagger to the shoreline, spent from a lifetime at sea.
Sh-sh-sh. Repeating the invocation to sleep,
I place him—still dreaming—
in the warm impression of a plover's nest.

Baby Siren Song

after the Harmony™ Medela Hand Pump

Port Melbourne, 2019

I assemble the pump in an office bathroom where the air discloses
a recent administration of hand soap: facsimile of bergamot,
buds on an unripe branch. The lemon-yellow lever initiates
a flesh seal. To manufacture a let-down is to re-imagine the baby,
to conjure her face, the bright rings of her irises, to be shunted
in the other direction: a dark green bay, shoreline of crushed pink
shells, foam-licked eddies. The *Spirit* docked and vacant before
a girl cradling her warm bundle of chips. The ocean moves
in a spritzy, roundabout way, with or against industry.
Reluctant drag amongst application's thrum: ever-present
is the temperate, electrical urging of a server room. A pitched voice
beyond the cubicle offers tea or coffee at the same time
I hear a baby cry. Then the milk flows, violet-tinged, primed
for the siren who produced the song. I twist close the lid, store
the bottle in an insulated lunch bag. Later, at my desk, I turn
my head towards the clamour of trapped seawater, her infant beak.
My chest rising—as it must—to her thunderous salt-call.

The Alligator

The
subject
line of the
email
from my
son's　　daycare reads:
Drone over　　*toddler yard.*
Anxiety　　flares its
little blue　　flames in
my blood-　　stream as I
scan the body　　text. *A low-*
flying drone　　*was reported*
over the toddler　　*yard at lunch-*
time today.　　*We brought the*
children inside. Some were
frightened. Police have been
notified & are investigating.
In the Everglades, a gator
is filmed catching, then
eating, a drone.　I too
would not hesitate to snatch
those junk birds out of the
warm sky, to crush their
warring wings between
my muscled jaws. Like an
ancient dragonfly whose
thatched eyes glare in
every direction, the drone-
over-toddler-yard would
atone for its intrusion in
the dark pit of my belly,
the same place where my
children were brewed. Alas
my reflexes are not what
they used to be. I write back,
thanks Julie for letting me
know. I want to leap, to tear
something up, to put my body
on the line. Instead I return to
my work, the words on screen
tethered to my fingers hovering
over　keys. More dragonflies. For
a　moment I am as still as a rep-
tile half-sunk in cool, green
water. One day our time will come.

The Cholmondeley Ladies

after "The Cholmondeley Ladies" c.1600–10

Sisters do not sit like this   like glass objects, grafted
to a single trunk. Neat as   Fell type. The truth is we
bled for the name: Cholm   ondeley. We met on the day
we wed those Ch-men, sh   eathed in white, spitting
vows: I ___ take you ___   ___ take me ___ & death
will not part us. Crossing   the threshold, they took
our faces, fashioned them   into hearts. Pallid ancestry,
shriek of thigh bone & clav   icle. Behold us! The wom
en halved & doubled: now   two (2) peas in a pod. One
(1) pair of silver slippers. O   ur children, lambent silk-
worms, born in the same h   our of the same day of the
same month of Cholmondel   ey blood – yes, Cholmondoley
blood – can you believe it   ? We cannot will not, yet
swaddle them still in red.   Baby girls, we hold them close,
whisper: you are without   equal, singular as sea life
& river stone. Do not belie   ve the Ch-men who paint
you & do not love you. We   know, we know. Becoming
Cholmondeley: a curse, we   know, a stunt, a black hoax.

The Harvest

after Adam Meyer's 'De wreedheid van de Zaandammer stier, 1647' (1756–1791)

The baby enters the world mid-flight.
Over soured ground, a harvest trampled
beyond sense,
           she is falling
into the body's small basket
like a wingless angel feeling her way into light.

A horn is living bone encased in keratin,
scalpel-sharp. Pinned beside an errant kite,
suspended over bull and dying man,
the mother flies despite the heaviness of her skirts,
considers her terrible gift—red stretch,
           child swimming into breath—and reaches out.

The uncut cord tugged free of its anchor,
a small body tumbles
untethered and without sound, through
           an astonished outline of clouds.

Note
Meyer's illustration depicts an accidental caesarean birth by bull goring.

A Platter / Love is

unfoiling a silver three-
cornered cheese, arranging fruit on bunny plate—
cut apple, green pear. In a shallow bowl

plums stewed ruby-pink. Crackers, wafers,
puffs of marbled rice. Bread sliced along the grain.
On each cut square a smaller square, unsalted.

Your chair set high and open like a throne.
I offer up cooked oats in coloured spoons,
a boiled egg with the yellow removed.

My quick hands learn slicing and scooping,
prospecting, proffering—anticipating labours,
each a small, vivid platter.

Two Cities

The city is an affluence of birds feathered in fair weather.
In scented streets we observe the heavy lifting of bees,
insects inculcating the earth. Garden sun skinks vanish
when we fall into step. A ready reckoner for human heat,
each morning I tongue creamy plastic, open a weather app
for clues. The sky holds no mystery—a swatch of Resolute Blue.

Impossible not to see flowers in all things—pavement gum,
electric toothbrush head, thumbprints in the hand's tacky vase.
On my desk, day-old coffee blooms fawn roses. I spill
the frowsty petals before I take a test, marvel at the body's quick wit.

Now light is trickling out as if there is a leak in the sky.
Stranded in a grainy boat, nausea hands me my own head
to heave-ho. In tap water I taste the Harbour, its silky steel,
sleek seals. I crave bitterest lemon, tart yellow sodas, salt on toast
to appease the serious crumb of you. At night I dream
of carbohydrates, flat streets, melaleuca exfoliating
on nature strips ruled by noisy miners. The road unspooling

like a black daisy as we return home by the sun-bitten highway,
every exit to a service station a pregnant pause. Soon the view
will be so far behind us we'll forget there ever was a bridge
stamping its concrete into blue restless water.

Remnants [Morning Walk]

after Karike Ashworth's 'Who Gives a Crap' (2021–2022)

Springtime: panicles of crimped, white flowers.
Caressed, discarded by wind. Down the street
we walk our infants, a flurry of light. Bright-
eyed, they are taking it all in: red car, white car.
Clouds nursing sky back to blue. A body
crumples when it moves. We've been working
the night shift. The day shift, too. Longest shift
of our lives. Fatigue creases our smiles: seams
exposed. We say: *take care!* We mean: *give it up!*
Children form committees to restore wind-torn
petals. We collect and salvage. Slowly, we recover.

Light on Water [Sound on]

after Jule Pokinghorne's 'The Swimming Lesson' (2021)

When light and water conspire, we know
we must swim up to where sound ripples out.

When light reverberates, flecks itself softly
through a glistening wave, a child's voice can be heard

calling clearly through the din of green water.
Sound and light converge to wash away a perimeter.

In the eaves of sound and light, I swim you: small shock-
wave. A splash resounds. Buoyed, unbodied:

in water's bright turbulence joy rises briskly,
breaks through a surface like light at daybreak.

Felling

Breath-
> less, you are hauled to the brink—

slick, red scarp.

Silent until a small wail
> diverts the partition,

dislodges the stone in my throat.

Scalpel reverses, flesh and muscle
> re-greet. No incision

when you land on my chest's warm want.

caedō meaning to cut / hew / fell //
> Like trees

we breathe in each other's air.

Lives Streaming

A woman in official green confirms *we are live*
from *Hippo Cove* where Fiona—fraction of pink hip,
apple of her mother's eye—circuits the anchorage.

A small-town star even before the zoo closes
and children surveil it for signs of life.
We ask, *where is Fiona going?* Fiona is ribboning out

like rose-coloured ice to a galaxy of housebound children.
My daughter, possessing none of Fiona's porpoise ease,
shifts in her chair. I fill a sink with hot water, lemon-

scented dish soap. Off-screen, Bibi spans the false bank,
keeping tabs. Below her, a fleet of tilapia scrub the tank blue.
When I tap to pause, Fiona stops too: she has reached

the world-thick glass. In a certain light we can see
the oiled pulse of our fingertips on the warm screen, vacant
hours expanding like black sedges through which Fiona must,

at times, eye the unfamiliar sky. So what if this life resembles
a cave? Nothing like Bibi imagined when she first felt
Fiona flicker: a dream of fish. Now she is learning

to forgive the cloud its biting rains. I know I am projecting
as I wipe down crusted tabletops, return bowls to cupboards,
flatware to drawers. From the laptop a zookeeper laughs:

Fiona makes a splash. Whether earned or inherited, rage
becomes the mother's mantle. Bibi shakes it off as she enters
ferried cold, begins a second act of displacement:

through her legs, through her stomach's powerful bulk,
she is transposing sunlight from water to air.

The Salience Network
[Street Scenes, Heidelberg]

We are walking daily now. We are stepping out at the inter-
    section of Cape and Brown where a bristling fir tree is
scrubbing tense from the sky. Presently I've never seen
    so many walkers, so many dogs on leashes and sun-glossed

puffer jackets swimming in autumn's glare. My son
    in a stroller, bald head capped in out-of-season sunhat,
sporty in white-and-navy stars. My daughter on foot,
    hopping and idling by pink-hearted daisies.

In the allotted hour, the cones of the fir tree—once
    slim green hats—fatten into brown globes, expansive
as eyes. Like reverse fireworks, a flock of cockatoos
    descend from the sky to plunder the woody scales,

shred spiked branches. Fanned bracts over blue-
    toned pavement where we begin our morning walk
and needles rain down upon the heads of passers-by.
    We are walking and I am scanning footpaths

for trip hazards, driveways for reversing cars. Leathery,
    dogbane oleander leaves. Chalk-coated berries
appealing in purple skin. Prepped for danger—
    future's proof in the quality of my attention.

Uncertainty is unbearable until I take it out for a walk.
    Like a dog I am showing it a garden of artificial grass.
Next a garden of satiny acanthus. Variegated lawns.
    Vegetable patches scrabbled with herbs, starred lettuce

hearts, Italianate latticework. Everything a threat.
 Everything real and growing sideways. Our neighbour's
fir tree so close to the house that its branches press
 the fringed glass like a heartsick giant looking in.

Avoiding people, their radial breath and quilted jackets
 exhaling on the verge. I want to be a myna marking
territory with plumed fisticuffs, rinsing air with song. I eye
 my intention. Bare teeth beneath non-woven fabric.

Wearing a mask I can still taste cold and sweet. Last year
 is over. The year before last is over, is returning now
in streets that curve like wood after years at sea. At the peak
 of Hawdon, the vista spans the Mercy—crossed,

brushed white—where my children were lifted from me
 in blue-lit clouds of relief. Year of the ground glass
lung. We are grinding scales and bracts beneath our boots.
 We are watching a magpie come to rest on the branch

of a tall candlebark, honeycomb a sweet tune. Next year
 a truck will misread the road and reverse into this tree,
splitting its trunk like parting the earth. A man will be
 trapped beneath a halo of muted leaves while the driver

sits wailing on the curb. The driver is wrapping his arms
 around his torso as if he is shattered timber. We watch
the splinters rain down upon the heads of passers-by.
 The streetscape is changing again. We intrude like thoughts,

plant the wrong things. Vines imperil saplings. Dog-like,
   I detect menace beyond a fenceline. Beginning
at the fir tree which shakes its sharp eyes, gathers its birds,
   we are walking the street we will walk again.

The Mask

after Lai-Tze Fan, Anne Sullivan and Anastasia Salter's 'Masked Making' (2021)

Pinch the wire over the bridge.
Walk with the cloth that covers a mouth
to a field where the grass has yellowed
despite recent rain. Unstrap the child
from the stroller. Invite her to run.
Pinch the wire while you put a hat on the baby
strapped to your chest. Breathe in the cloth
dyed a floral print. Taste its weave:
pink peonies where a mouth would be.
Pass the child an apple. When the sky clears
sunlight moves like water over yellow grass.
A phrase will spring to mind: *en plein air*.
Years since you studied the language
but in this moment of dislocation it returns
like a long-lost cat found pinched from weather:
slimmer, muscled, purring with pleasure.
En plein air the baby begins to fuss.
En plein air a kite and another child enter the scene.
The children regard each other with wonder.
Pinch the bridge. A mother waves.
Do not approach but return a salute and smile
beneath the patch where pink peonies bloom.

Letters to Jocelyn

after 'Imitating B's Toddler Style (24th / 26th March 2022)' by Jocelyn Allen

I say, *would it be alright if I wrote about you in an ekphrastic way?*

No one would read it, probably. Or a select few only. And, ekphrastically speaking, a poem is not a mirror—it responds, it does not represent. But if it does (represent) then it is only by matter of degree. A filament of light is an approximation of colour, etc.

If you say blue, I say _____.

Allow me to be declarative. The bowl is blue. I admire the artistic drive of mothers. And the other drive: to simultaneously tame, and surrender to, the toddler spirit. How we all visit the same hill to answer the question:

> *do I want to die here?*

Figuratively, of course. The lesson all expectant mothers are taught: choose your battles wisely.

This is the hill.

In the photo
> a frayed tea towel, chequered green, adorns your chest like a cotton breastplate. You wear it as B wore it, which is as a knight might wear it—the female kind—standing before us on the eve of encounter.

You bear witness to your child and reflect her serious gaze back on to the world. I want to say, this is some feat. I once tried to describe C in the form of a sestina and look where it got me!

When I tell H he cannot XYZ, I find my hill and fall to my knees. The grass below is cold and wet like the black nose of a dog. H cries and cries and I feel the tears running over his perfect round cheeks as if they are my own.

*

Why does early parenthood feel so much like weathering? Storms, yes, but also the doldrums. The sea flat as a disc, the sky blazing blue and not a wrinkle of a breeze to enliven the sails. You'd know this, Jocelyn, because you, too, had a pandemic baby. Two pandemic babies.

We lived inside our houses the way soft-bodied creatures live inside their shells (sometimes I still live this way).

Now, like then, we communicate via a messaging app in the style of long-distance penpals. Without distance, we might not write at all. We might have coffee together instead.

Dear Jocelyn, I see our lives running together as two country roads, the air cold and dark and sweet. When I write in the day, you answer at night, which is your day, too. Unless the children are not sleeping and we write at odd hours like pre-predawn.

*

Dear Jocelyn, isn't all poetry epistolary?

I want to ask, *how would you describe the light?*

What I am really asking is, *how should I describe the light?*

I have no real knowledge of photography. What I can say about (your) light is that

　　　1) it is unflinching, and

　　　2) it turns limbs into water.

Jocelyn, how is B? And is L sleeping better now? She was teething last time we spoke.

Also: how do you withstand the gaze of others when it is just you in the frame in a stained blue dress

　　　　　　　　and the light is unflinching?

When I look at your 'Portrait of a Mother' photos, I see that planning and spontaneity are two sides of the same coin. That the hard edge of a creative life is care—

And perhaps this is the crux of the matter. It takes time to feed and dress and bathe and sing to sleep a small child. So we test our wills not against our children but against time, which grows as thin and expansive as a seafloor.

　　　　　　　　　　Is this the hill?

　　　　　　　　　*

There is a kind of light that leaves nothing untouched (you know it well). It takes time to cultivate this light, to bring to life the steely nerves of a child, the playfulness of mothers.

And still the Internet teems with people who say, *I see you.*

Dear Jocelyn, your work reminds me of the unassailable fact: only when light passes through the eye do we see each other.

The Warning

floats in shallow seawater—bowl of laced pudding,
lavish banquet of arms. A bubble of surprise

as the ripple's centre bleeds its blueness into the tide.
H reaching for its elastic crown before I grab his hand,

rig his small body to the shelf of my hip. He sits
instinctively, sweetly—soft tuft of grass on a plateau.

The beach swells with lolloping sound—lightning
a quick poison if we're to believe the sky's violet blooms.

Heads bowed, I scramble with H in my arms over dunes
roped together by invasive marram. Fear dangling

like a dead thing. When we reach the gravel car park—
shelter of flat earth, piked saltbush—the air grows warm

and heavy. A hand on my shoulder. I anchor H
to a Britax Safe-n-Sound, five-point harness moving

like the orange arms of a sea-star. My terror, so often rising,
transmutes into laughter. I am showing him

how to discard fear like a coat in unseasonable warmth.
Below us the ocean is in thrall, dead or alive

with silent bells expiring in shuttered blue light.

Visions

It begins with one tau emerald, dead
    on the screen door. Nose-diver, weighted

dart. Then another—alive, hovering over
    my daughter's head like an emergency.

For a moment it appears to land on her hair
    cross-hatched like a river's tan bank

until a shift of her body, of light, is seized
    in a pair of compound eyes. Resolution

exchanged for relational, wide-angle vision—
    a message to move on. In a week made strange

by weather, we see the garden become air-
    space. Sunlight vents serrated mandibles,

crowns lawns in chiton. Decline so common-
    place we doubt at first our eyes, deny

this iridescence of wings, abundant swarm.
    How did we overlook nymphs stirring

for months in aquatic cellars, busting out
    of temporary suits every other night?

And where is our nearest body of water?
    We walk the block seeking the source before

heat returns us—fractious, empty-handed—
    to the question, *what else did we miss?*

Urgent as a dragonfly's predacious flight.

Screensaver

My mother's vials are small, very neat. The ants
glimmer, a mineral shine, each leg intact and so petite
that they appear fabricated: miniatures rinsed

in black ink. At the university she is a student
forever in need of a photocopier. Her charges return
to a metal cabinet with a tidy clink before we enter

a room where computers sleep, green-hued in rows
of fevered hardware, silent but for the grand cases
that hum and broil in the heat of memory.

I spend the hour rotating on swivel chairs, rolling
tethered mice across soft tar. Patience is its own reward:
sit still long enough and one-by-one the screens explode

into millions of stars hurtling like weightless bodies
on water. Edge-less, infinite. A galaxy of luminescent ants
no longer point-mounted on pins but surging out

on vast tides. I sit transfixed by the display, unable to move
or avert my gaze until a larger sun enters my orbit—
my mother with her printed stack, calling me away.

The Grasshopper

has no weight when it lands
on a sun-baked blade.
My daughter names it *hop-grass*.

Remember last year? A sunset
so indisputably purple it crashed through cloud,
turned whole sheets into rain.
Our small patch fragrant with flowering parsley,
rigid seeds soaked yellow-green.

Today the sun is an orange disc.
Tomorrow the sun will be an orange disc
clarified by smoke. Tell me: if I store
the heft of memory in water,
will a long drought erase it?

The hazard begins in the lung's soft lobes.
We measure the extent of disaster
in burnished air, russet tones, charred animal fur.
No choice but to remain indoors
where we breathe in the rich polymers
of toy animals balanced on her bed.
Hand-eye is the name we give an invisible line
but here it goes on forever.

I take photos of the garden, my daughter
a colour wheel in flight. The photos
smell of nothing—not even smoke.

The sun beating down on a green parallelogram
reveals a solution in contraction,

in the springiness that comes from muscle
and play, which is a kind of plain sight.

The novel *hop-grass*
flickers over yellow lawn.
I stuff memory into language, apply heat to set.

The Lemon Tree

is unburdening. Curled leaves drift over mulched earth
until its branches are bald to the morning sun.

A fissure in the trunk, no wider than a fingernail, indicates
something. Someone is eating it from the inside.

I fear it is a nest of pincer-teeth. The tree sickened
the week we moved in and a question takes root—did we bring

the pincer-teeth with us? I see them nestled in the fibres
of a cardboard box, in damp packets of grains, marching

to the host whose oiled leaves plot a map on the breeze.
We know we have a problem but our hands have lost expertise

correcting decay. A harbinger of something. I stop sleeping,
am hungry all the time. Are we the pincer-teeth?

You close the blinds to shield our eyes from the appalling pallor
of dead wood. *Baby,* you whisper, *forget the tree. It was dying*

the day we moved in. When I close my eyes, I hear them chewing.
One thousand pincer-teeth phantoms. The bark turning soft

in our mouths.

Reflections on Yellow

I celebrate the obsolescence of nine am over buttered toast.
After taking C to school, I drive H to the park

where magpies greet each other from the ground like neat Romeos.
Light filters butter-yellow through branches. We encounter

the day as a verge of bright flatweed soaking up the sun's neglect.
H wanders with me like a cloud—casting shadows, collecting water.

We need new names for work, I say aloud to no one. My ex-job
goes on making things without me. My hours fill with larger acts

of creation: words spoken, repeated; H filing away whole swathes
of language so that soon complete sentences arrive on his tongue.

Still, there are mornings that feel like the citrus fade of an old bruise:
the cat yowls, the children fight, cereal spills its flaky gold across

the unwashed floor. Lemon vis-à-vis lemonade. Still, a vivid inner life
becomes available in the soft light of three pm when we walk to

and from school. In this quiet wedge of an afternoon, H drags his feet,
directs my attention to a crack in the pavement. The beetle—glint

of amber—ambling on furred feet. We watch without speaking.
Silence proves golden, reveals the serious business of being alive.

Amulets

after 'an amuletic necklace worn to cure sore throats', London (1914),
Wellcome Collection

To protect a child's throat from diphtheria's grey taint,
the necklace performs its function in clear or coloured glass:
each bead an appeal in a circle of green, brown and pink;
a plea held together by a simple brass clasp.

In the breath of a glass blower, then warmed against the neck
of its wearer, the beads grow alive to danger.
It is easy for me to pity the one who bestowed the gift
until I remember the name I gave my daughter. *Clover*

to confer good fortune, a charm against calamity or casual
bad luck. Each time I speak her name, I weave a brief spell:
clipped syllables hang in the air like a curl of green smoke.
Fortune resides in apotropaic names–the bitter taste

of effort and love. We detect danger on the tongue, disguise
our children in disaster's intricate language. *Inferno. Inundation.*
In the lungs where we practise the power of wishful thinking,
we voice our invocations, pit hope against hope.

And if nothing else works, perhaps we will return
to those earth-hued beads cooling the skin of our throats.
Not to safeguard the body from sickness
but particulate matter: the hazardous atoms of smoke.

On This Day Ninth of August Twenty Twenty Three

a promotional email recommends a book
to help me reclaim my authenticity. And yet
I'd felt the hard edge of my authentic self

only an hour ago, sweating alone on a dirt track
slicked by winter sunlight, breath tangling in the spool
of my throat. It was pressed against the air

thick with bees and pollen. Gold swirling in a pan.
Mid-run, I stopped by the flowering wattle, angled
my phone to snap snap the cheerleading blooms.

My authenticity said, *you want to keep this.*
This is who I am: always giving myself small gifts.

~

Any good book on authenticity begins with anger.
To come into anger is to anneal the self.
To feel unyielding. The hot bright kernel of an outburst

as certain as it is unbidden: turning me inside out.
At night, small and not-small grievances seep like cold water
into the loamy surface of my dreams,

transmute into blades or blunt objects. To sublimate
rage is to divert it back into the body.
A frustrated child, I would bite my own hand.

Tooth marks in skin gleam like arrowed apples.

~

Case studies

i.

> A celebrated writer. A derisive poem about a woman desiring
> a pregnancy and a husband with fast cars. I check the
> publication date: late-2000s. I let this rankle me. I spit the
> poem out and save the woman from the sneer.

ii.

> A common dream: I am driving a fast car but the brake
> pedal has come loose, has dissolved in sleep like sugar in
> the blood. My foot searches empty space, presses down on
> air. I feel free. Feather-light. Only when I plough into traffic
> do I wake.

iii.

> At the women's soccer match, a man behind me screams,
> *get up*, to a player on the ground. I want to turn around and
> shove him so hard that his sternum breaks. In my head I
> snarl, *get down*. I want to call him *maggot*. Who does anyone
> think they are?

iv.

> In sleep my son kicks like a dancer. When he wakes before
> dawn he tells me his good dream. *I dreamed about the forest.*
> We lie in blue light as trees sigh softly around us, notional
> as numbers.

~

I love my children so much it feels like breathing
with one hundred mouths. Oxygenated, mineralised.
Rich as a mountain seam. From the minute

my firstborn bursts onto the scene, a brisk division:
heart, then brain. Sinking into wet pine bark
at the playground, I explain to a friend how each morning

I split my mind neatly in two, cantaloupe-style. One half
I hand to my daughter, the other half to my son.
She does not ask, *what about you?* She knows

this equation can only be solved by experimental physicists,
other poets. A better question: is it possible
to remain authentic while divided? Let me argue the affirmative:

after all, we speak with the company of two lungs.
Break the body open and the composition of breath remains
unchanged: fidelity to a remnant is nothing but faithful.

~

Running the narrow dirt track, I realise my bones
crave impact: the thrumming thwack of compacted earth.
To be repelled by the ground is sensational.

I stand before the wattle in pillowy florescence, breathe in
the heavy, honeyed air. My shadow doubled, dotted with
ants. I witness its flatness in parts. This body so far

has been death-defying. I can only love it with all my heart.

A Dish Best Served I

The woman arrives early—just as cool, blue light
streaks the pavement.
She needs no introduction. I show her to the kitchen
where she removes her chef-hat,
sheds the thin, gold rings from her fingers.

When she smiles, she is my mother; frowning,
my sister—the one who dished out
charred bones and obliterated potato, remnants
of a village from a dragon's tale.

The chef holds an apple to demonstrate a point.
It becomes clear she is here not to make or mend
but to teach. She explains that a recipe must be learned
the hard way, that truth is an extract like vanilla—
macerated, soaked in ethanol and water.

A silver cloche is lifted from my mind each time
she speaks. No need to write it down—lessons gleam,
evident as globed peaches from a tin.

A Dish Best Served II

1. Slice forgiveness, the still-warm loaf, with a serrated blade; serve with a square of cold butter.
2. Desire, a blue-speckled egg, is best swallowed whole.
3. Fear should be plated in long grass beneath a baleful moon.
4. Kindness in earthenware, unwashed.
5. No utensils are required for largesse, only a soft mouth.
6. Boil contempt until it resembles a tooth. Present on a bed of greenest samphire.
7. Wrap old hurts in vine leaves and simmer from one season to the next. Eat when tender.
8. Longing, shame—mealy, only half-dead—will catch in the throat.
9. Wash everything down with yellow nectar, the plum-heart of pity, and;
10. Never forget it was made with love.

What to Forget When You're Expecting

I. FIRST THINGS FIRST

Put down the birthing manual, the melon-heavy book
of directives: a poem is enough.
This and your mother's living ghost will cleave
a space for nuance, air enough to breathe.

II. YOUR PREGNANCY LIFESTYLE

Acclimate in brown-tiled bathrooms.
Expect to misspend weeks studying the shine of basins,
sipping water that tastes like the boiled sea.
Press beneath your tongue a square of ginger,
dark and sugared like tree sap, and hum.
Eat salt. Eat the pickle, drink the brine.

What you put in your body is interesting to everyone:
expect looks. Expect hands bold and opaque
like brass work. The tall midwife will glide
her Doppler, dolphin-like, over the gleaming dome of you.
A baby is shaped on currents of grey static.
It sounds like *wow-wow-wow-wow*.

III. ALL ABOUT PUSHING AND DELIVERY

When the body's hip-shaped roadblocks obstruct,
metaphors may assist: in theatre, a blue sheet
is a hitched tent. Doctors are gowned archaeologists
on a dig. Replace *caesarean section* with *excavation*
and you may share in the excitement

as the baby is lifted from you, silver-skinned,
an intact amphora or bag of precious coins.

Expect to tremble like the earth. Your greatest fear:
that she will slip from your arms and dissolve
like a dream against the hard, washed ground.

IV. AFTER THE BABY IS BORN

She will anticipate nothing but goodwill:
love ushered like a ferry over water,
a window filling with light.

V. WHAT YOU MAY BE WONDERING ABOUT

You must forget the sun will not last forever.
4.5 billion years, give or take, before it swells
and contracts, turns red-then-white-hot.
Eventually it will eat the Earth, strip the ice from Pluto.
Advice from relatives, other mothers, that woman
at the bus stop, accumulates like rind on fruit:
coarse and orbital. It is expressed as *breathe*.

Breathe: your baby will not live to see our best star die.
Your baby is here. A ship set on a chanced breeze.
Breathe. Breathe. Breathe. Breathe. Breathe.
You have something. Take another breath.

Note
The lines that make up the subheadings of each section are taken from various
editions of Heidi Murkoff's What to Expect When You're Expecting.

Acknowledgements

Three lines from 'Woman to Child' by Judith Wright, published in *Collected Poems* (2016), are reproduced with permission from HarperCollins Publishers Australia Pty Limited.

Two lines from the poem beginning 'You kiss the forehead – to wipe away fear' by Marina Tsvetaeva, translated by Michael N. Naydan and published in *Marina Tsvetaeva: The essential poetry* (2015), are reproduced with permission from Michael M. Naydan and Glagoslav Publications.

A number of poems in this collection have been published previously: 'Megafauna' in Westerly (2023); 'Visions' in Plumwood Mountain Journal (2023); 'The Salience Network [Street Scenes, Heidelberg]' in Cordite Poetry Review (2023); 'Night Notes' in Island (2023); 'The Human Body' in Island (2023); 'Screensaver' in foam:e (2023); 'The Green Wedge' in Island (2022); 'Personal Slalom' in Meanjin (2022); 'The Cholomondeley Ladies' in Rabbit (2018); 'Ode to a BabyCentre Forum' in Rabbit (2023); 'The Transfer' and 'Two Cities' in Liquid Amber Press' The Poetry of Home (2023); 'Fool at Perigee' in Going Down Swinging (2023); and 'I Cutlass Spent Days with an X' in Cordite Poetry Review (2024). 'The Wing' and 'What to Forget When You're Expecting' were longlisted and first published in the 2023 University of Canberra Vice-Chancellor's International Poetry Prize. Thank you to the dedicated editors and staff of these publications.

Thank you to the team at UWAP, especially Kate Pickard and Lauren Pratt, for your guidance and support. And many thanks to Lisa White for creating the perfect cover. Much of this book was written as I was on maternity leave at Cambridge University Press, Australia. Thank you to the colleagues and friends I have worked with over many years at CUP, especially Kim Armitage. Other poems were written during my first year of a PhD in Creative Writing at Monash University. Many thanks to Dr Simone Murray for your encouragement and astute feedback.

Heartfelt thanks to Kirra Turner for your unwavering friendship and for inspiring the poem, 'The Scar'. For the conversations that have made me think more deeply about writing, life, parenting, creativity, and art, thank you Samantha Allemann, Alex Chambers, Vilija Stephens, Jocelyn Allen. Thank you to the educators who have cared for my children and given me time to write.

To my mothers, Genevieve Mead and Mary McKinnon, my brother, Sebastian Lynch, and my husband, Joe Curtis: thanks for never doubting. And thank you, forever and always, Clover and Hugo Curtis-Mead. You are the reason this book exists.